Jewish songs
for C tuning ukulele

Ondřej Šárek

Contents

Copyright © 2013 Ondřej Šárek
All rights reserved.
ISBN-13: 978-1484899595
ISBN-10: 1484899598

Introduction

The ukulele managed to spread worldwide as well as Jewish music before. Moreover, Jewish music achieved to absorb different folk music, mostly European. For the reason you can meet here with beautiful melodies in minor, which are not scales preferred by ukulele playing.

Even more, I would like to emphasize that Jewish songs are often accompanied by Jewish liturgy. If you want to be more interested in Jewish music, it is suitable to get know something in this area.

You can find in book here 20 Jewish songs. Each song is arranged in two keys. What you need is to now your favorite key, maybe take a capo and start playing.

Capo

Songs in this book are recorded just in eight keys. If some of songs do not suit your voice range just to take capo and find a right position for you. In the following tab there are new keys that form when using a capo. I wrote them up to 5th fret however you can use it further.

	D minor	G minor	A minor	C major
1st fret	D# / E♭	G#/A♭	A# / B♭	C# / D♭
2nd fret	E	A	B	D
3rd fret	F	A# / B♭	C	D# / E♭
4th fret	F#/G♭	B	C# / D♭	E
5th fret	G	C	D	F

	F major	G major	D modal	G modal
1st fret	F#/G♭	G#/A♭	D# / E♭	G#/A♭
2nd fret	G	A	E	A
3rd fret	G#/A♭	A# / B♭	F	A# / B♭
4th fret	A	B	F#/G♭	B
5th fret	A# / B♭	C	G	C

How to read tablature

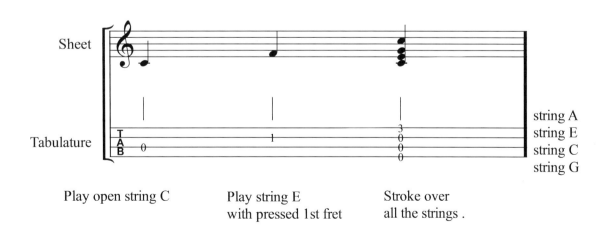

Sheet

Tabulature

string A
string E
string C
string G

Play open string C   Play string E   Stroke over
                          with pressed 1st fret   all the strings .

D minor

Adon Olam

arr: Ondřej Šárek

G minor

Adon Olam

arr: Ondřej Šárek

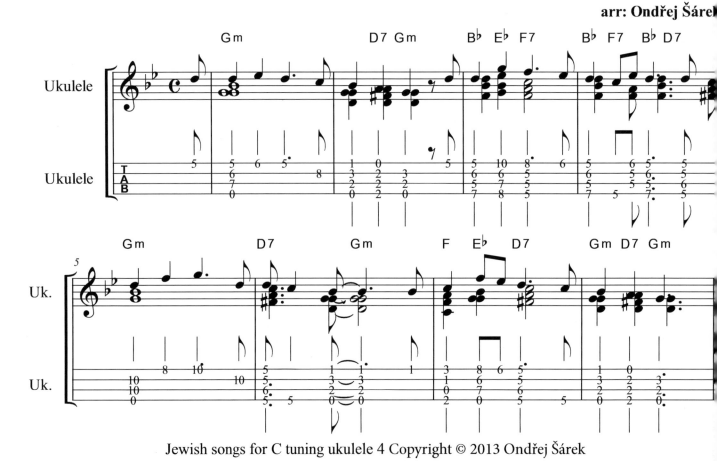

Amcha Jisrael

arr: Ondřej Šárek

A minor

D minor

Amcha Jisrael

arr: Ondřej Šárek

Artsa Alinu

arr: Ondřej Šárek

minor

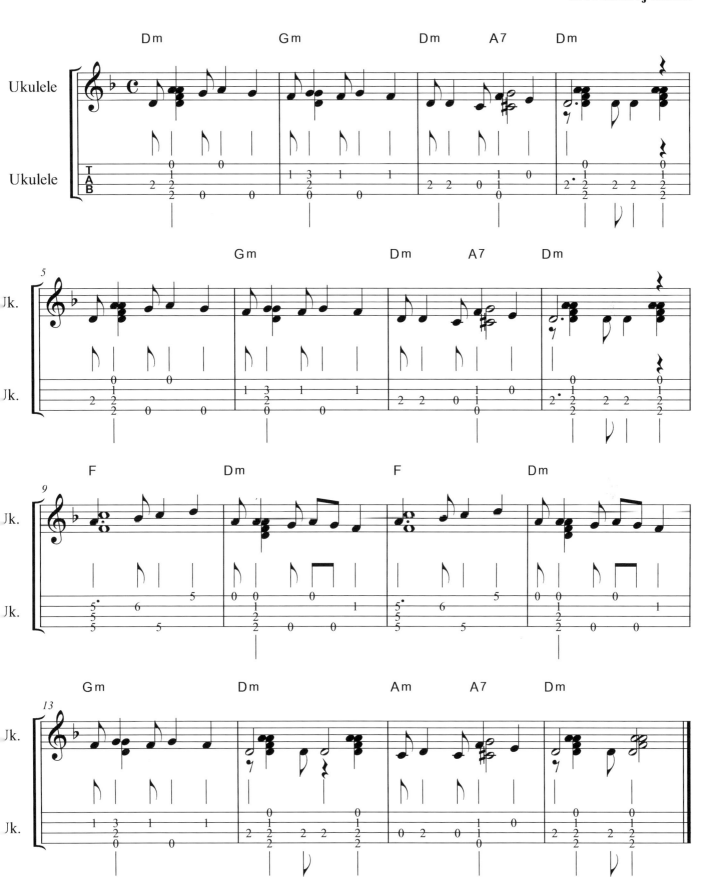

G minor

Artsa Alinu

arr: Ondřej Šárek

modal

Avinu Malkenu

arr: Ondřej Šárek

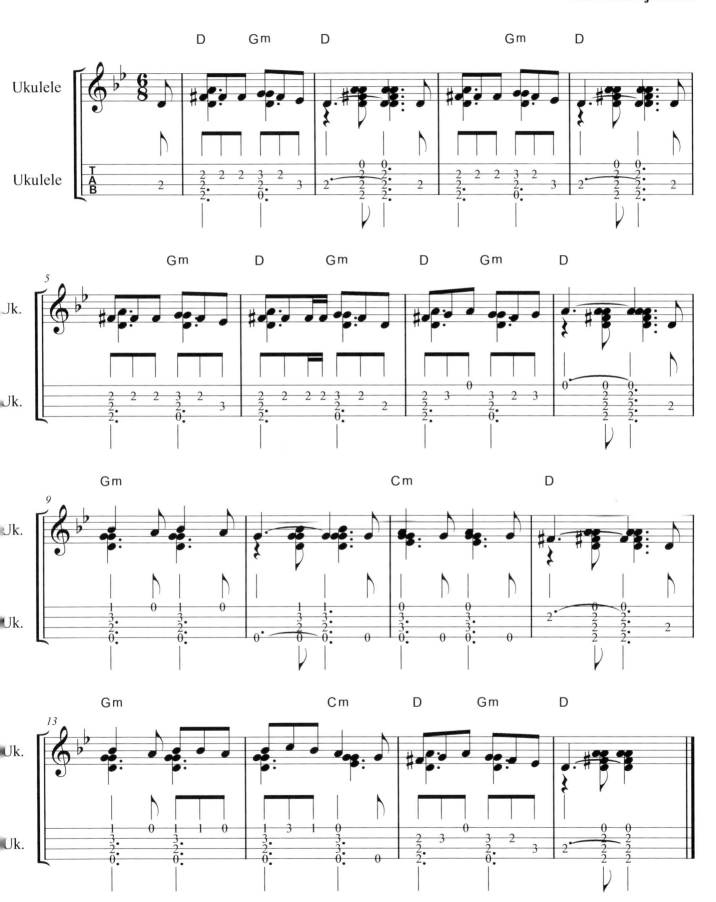

Avinu Malkenu

G modal

arr: Ondřej Šárek

Chiribim Chiribom

arr: Ondřej Šárek

Chiribim Chiribom

D minor

arr: Ondřej Šárek

C major

Dajejnu

arr: Ondřej Šárek

F major

Dajejnu

arr: Ondřej Šárek

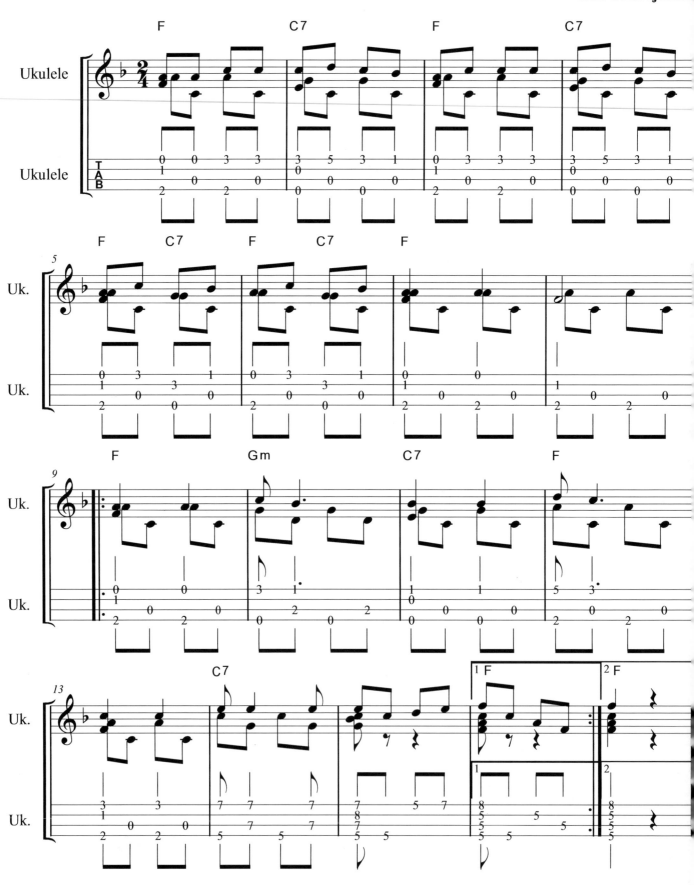

David Melech Yisrael

arr: Ondřej Šárek

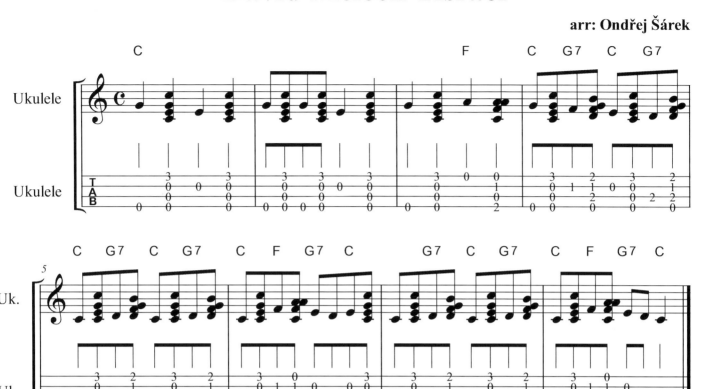

David Melech Yisrael

arr: Ondřej Šárek

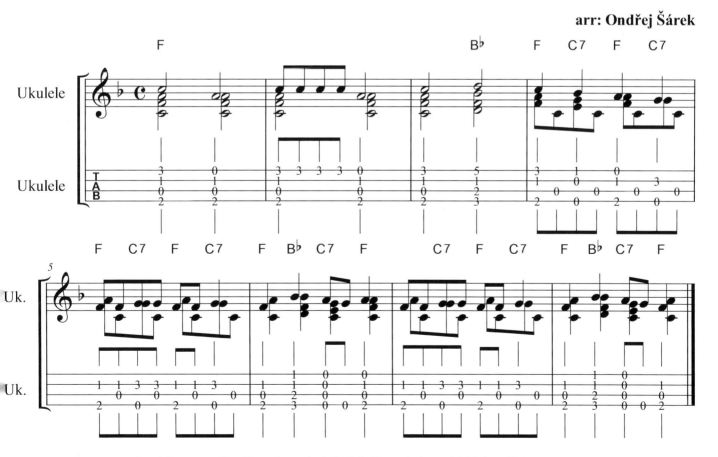

C major

Hanukkah, Hanukkah

arr: Ondřej Šárek

Jewish songs for C tuning ukulele 16 Copyright © 2013 Ondřej Šárek

Hanukkah, Hanukkah

arr: Ondřej Šárek

A minor

Hava Nagila

arr: Ondřej Šárek

Hava Nagila

D minor

arr: Ondřej Šáre

Hava Nagila

D minor

Hevenu Shalom Aleichem

arr: Ondřej Šáre

G minor

Hevenu Shalom Aleichem

arr: Ondřej Šáre

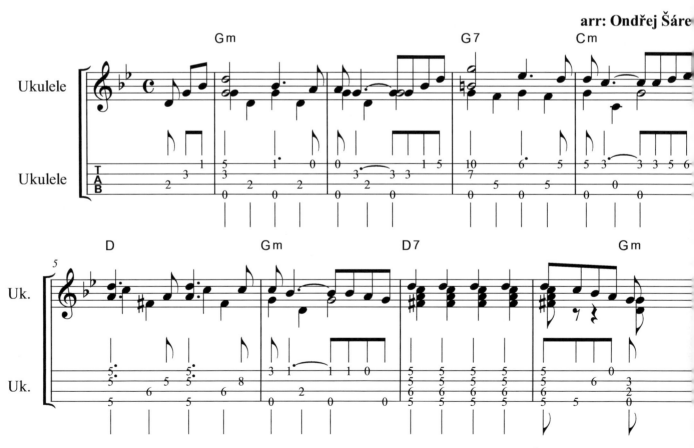

Hine Ma Tov

A minor

arr: Ondřej Šárek

Hine Ma Tov

D minor

arr: Ondřej Šárek

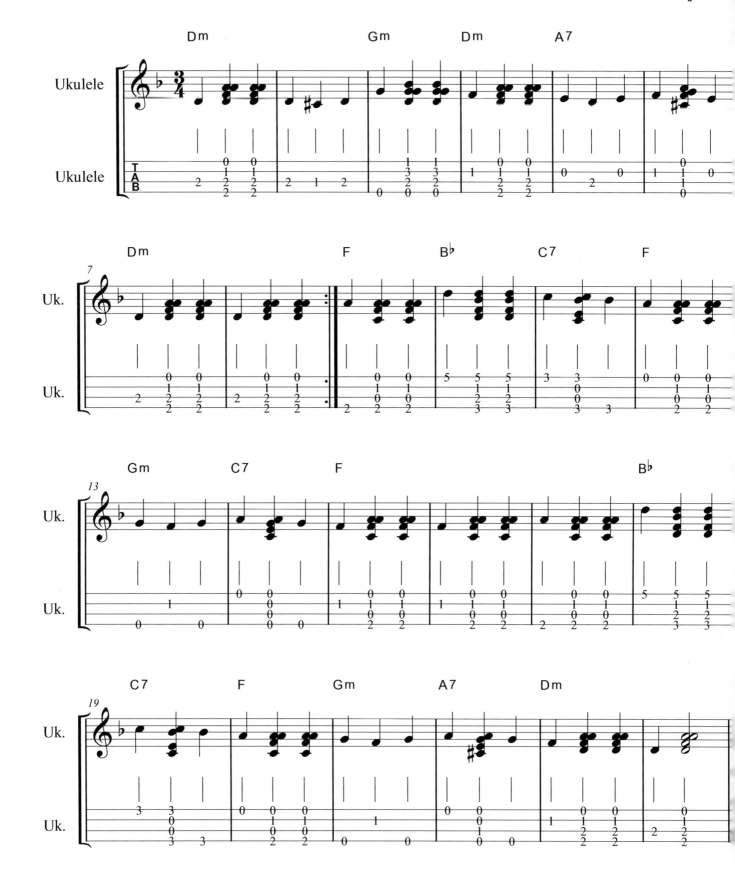

Chag Purim

A minor

arr: Ondřej Šárek

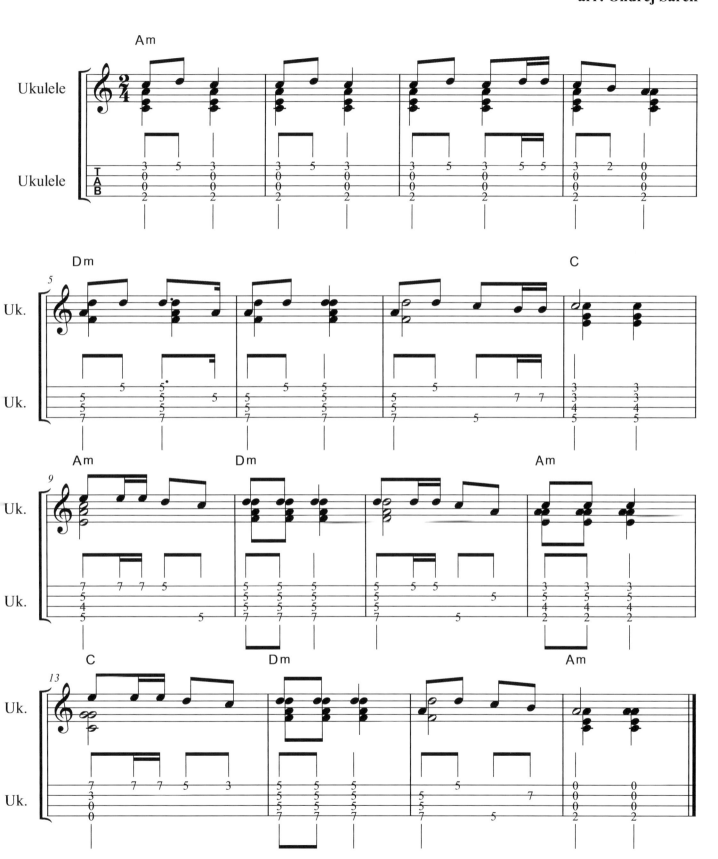

Chag Purim

D minor

arr: Ondřej Šárek

A minor

Kadesh Urchac

Kadesh Urchac

D minor

arr: Ondřej Šárek

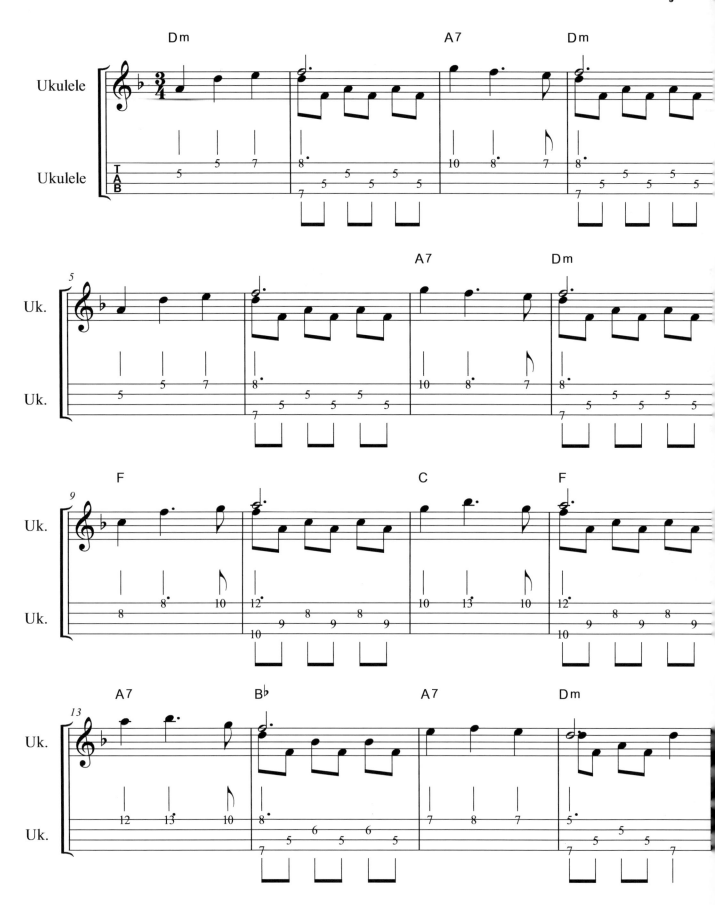

Ner Li

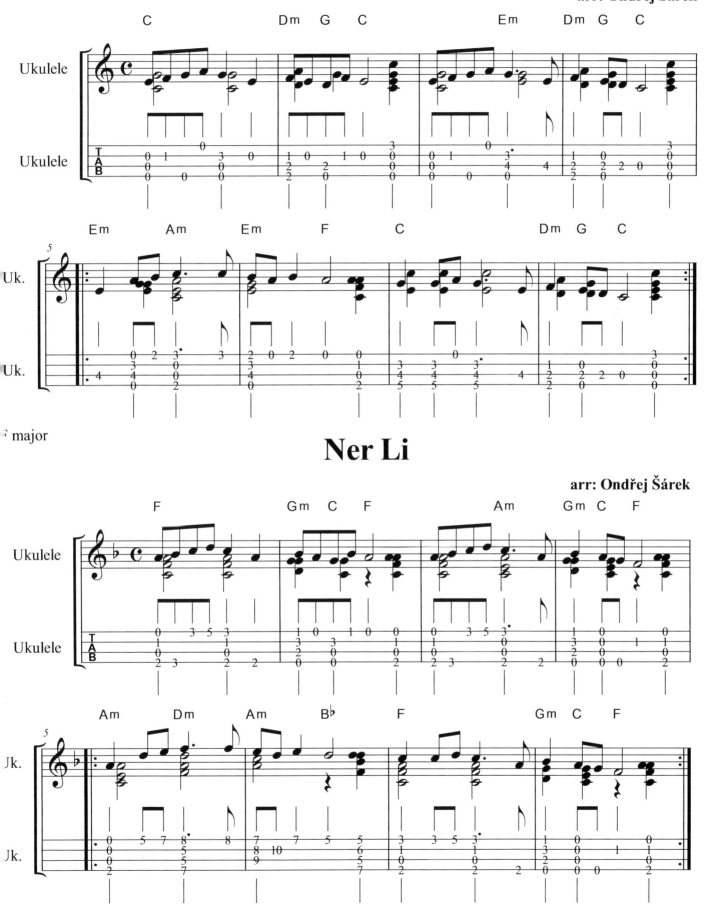

C major

Nerot Shabat

arr: Ondřej Šárek

Nerot Shabat

Nerot Shabat

F major

arr: Ondřej Šárek

Nerot Shabat

Shalom Chaverim

A minor

arr: Ondřej Šárek

Shalom Chaverim

D minor

arr: Ondřej Šárek

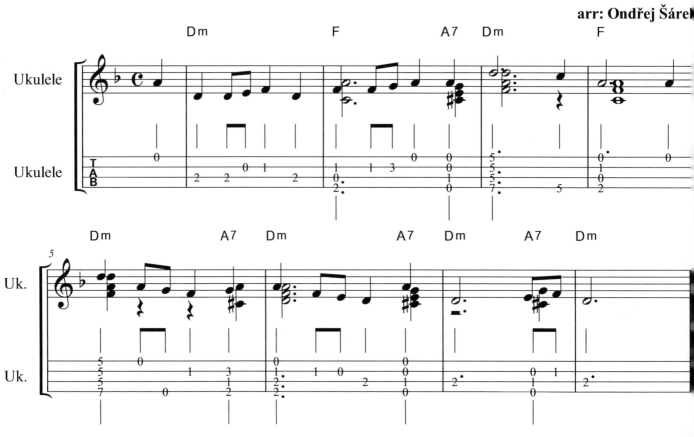

Sevivon

arr: Ondřej Šárek

D minor

Sevivon

G minor

arr: Ondřej Šárek

Shema Israel

arr: Ondřej Šárek

Tum Balalaika

D minor

arr: Ondřej Šárek

Tum Balalaika

G minor

arr: Ondřej Šárek

D minor

Yoshke Fort Avek

arr: Ondřej Šárek

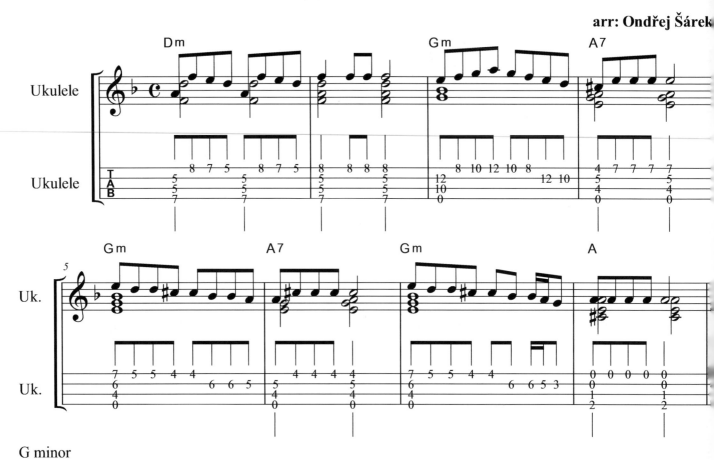

G minor

Yoshke Fort Avek

arr: Ondřej Šárek

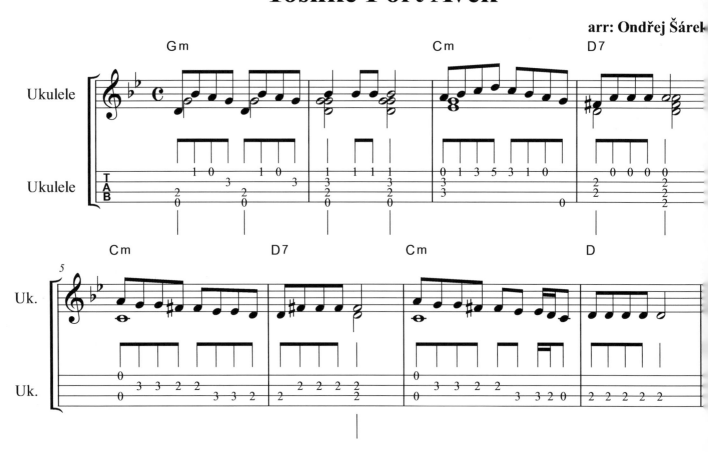

New Ukulele books

For C tuning ukulele
Classics for Ukulele (Mel Bay Publications)
Ukulele Bluegrass Solos (Mel Bay Publications)
Antonin Dvorak: Biblical Songs (CreateSpace Independent Publishing Platform)
Irish tunes for all ukulele (CreateSpace Independent Publishing Platform)
Gospel Ukulele Solos (CreateSpace Independent Publishing Platform)
Gregorian chant for Ukulele (CreateSpace Independent Publishing Platform)
The Czech Lute for Ukulele (CreateSpace Independent Publishing Platform)
Romantic Pieces by Frantisek Max Knize for Ukulele (CreateSpace Independent Publishing Platform)
Notebook for Anna Magdalena Bach and Ukulele (CreateSpace Independent Publishing Platform)
Open Tunings for Ukulel (Mel Bay Publications)
Robert Burns songs for ukulele (CreateSpace Independent Publishing Platform)
Jewish songs for C tuning ukulele (CreateSpace Independent Publishing Platform)

For C tuning with low G
Irish tunes for all ukulele (CreateSpace Independent Publishing Platform)
Gospel Ukulele low G Solos (CreateSpace Independent Publishing Platform)
Antonin Dvorak: Biblical Songs: for Ukulele with low G (CreateSpace Independent Publishing Platform)
Gregorian chant for Ukulele with low G (CreateSpace Independent Publishing Platform)
The Czech Lute for Ukulele with low G (CreateSpace Independent Publishing Platform)
Romantic Pieces by Frantisek Max Knize for Ukulele with low G (CreateSpace Independent Publishing Platform)
Notebook for Anna Magdalena Bach and Ukulele with low G (CreateSpace Independent Publishing Platform)
Robert Burns songs for ukulele with low G (CreateSpace Independent Publishing Platform)
Jewish songs for ukulele with low G (CreateSpace Independent Publishing Platform)

For Baritone ukulele
Irish tunes for all ukulele (CreateSpace Independent Publishing Platform)
Gospel Baritone Ukulele Solos (CreateSpace Independent Publishing Platform)
Antonin Dvorak: Biblical Songs: for Baritone Ukulele (CreateSpace Independent Publishing Platform)
Gregorian chant for Baritone Ukulele (CreateSpace Independent Publishing Platform)
The Czech Lute for Baritone Ukulele (CreateSpace Independent Publishing Platform)
Romantic Pieces by Frantisek Max Knize for Baritone Ukulele (CreateSpace Independent Publishing Platform)
Notebook for Anna Magdalena Bach and Baritone Ukulele (CreateSpace Independent Publishing Platform)
Robert Burns songs for Baritone ukulele (CreateSpace Independent Publishing Platform)
Jewish songs for baritone ukulele (CreateSpace Independent Publishing Platform)

For Baritone ukulele with high D
Jewish songs for baritone ukulele with high D (CreateSpace Independent Publishing Platform)

For 6 sting ukulele (Lili'u ukulele)
Gospel 6 string Ukulele Solos (CreateSpace Independent Publishing Platform)
Gregorian chant for 6 string Ukulele (CreateSpace Independent Publishing Platform)
Notebook for Anna Magdalena Bach and 6 string Ukulele (CreateSpace Independent Publishing Platform)
Robert Burns songs for 6 string ukulele (CreateSpace Independent Publishing Platform)

For Slide ukulele (lap steel ukulele)
Comprehensive Slide Ukulele: Guidance for Slide Ukulele Playing (CreateSpace Independent Publishing Platform)
Gospel Slide Ukulele Solos (CreateSpace Independent Publishing Platform)
Irish tunes for slide ukulele (CreateSpace Independent Publishing Platform)
Robert Burns songs for Slide ukulele (CreateSpace Independent Publishing Platform)

For D tuning ukulele
Skola hry na ukulele (G+W s.r.o.)
Irish tunes for all ukulele (CreateSpace Independent Publishing Platform)
Jewish songs for D tuning ukulele (CreateSpace Independent Publishing Platform)

Duets
Notebook for Anna Magdalena Bach, C tuning ukulele and C tuning ukulele (CreateSpace Independent Publishing Platform)
Notebook for Anna Magdalena Bach, C tuning ukulele and Ukulele with low G (CreateSpace Independent Publishing Platform)
Notebook for Anna Magdalena Bach, C tuning ukulele and Baritone ukulele (CreateSpace Independent Publishing Platform)
Notebook for Anna Magdalena Bach, Ukulele with low G and Ukulele with low G (CreateSpace Independent Publishing Platform)
Notebook for Anna Magdalena Bach, Ukulele with low G and Baritone ukulele (CreateSpace Independent Publishing Platform)
Notebook for Anna Magdalena Bach, Baritone ukulele and Baritone ukulele (CreateSpace Independent Publishing Platform)

New Anglo Concertina books

For C/G 30-button Wheatstone Lachenal System
Gospel Anglo Concertina Solos (CreateSpace Independent Publishing Platform)
Notebook for Anna Magdalena Bach and Anglo Concertina (CreateSpace Independent Publishing Platform)
Robert Burns songs for Anglo Concertina (CreateSpace Independent Publishing Platform)

Coming soon!
The Czech Lute for Anglo Concertina (CreateSpace Independent Publishing Platform)
Gregorian chant for Anglo Concertina (CreateSpace Independent Publishing Platform)

For C/G 20-button
Gospel C/G Anglo Concertina Solos (CreateSpace Independent Publishing Platform)
Robert Burns songs for C/G Anglo Concertina (CreateSpace Independent Publishing Platform)

Coming soon!
Gregorian chant for C/G Anglo Concertina (CreateSpace Independent Publishing Platform)

New Melodeon books

For G/C melodeon
Bass songbook for G/C melodeon (CreateSpace Independent Publishing Platform)

97360780R00024

Made in the USA
Middletown, DE
04 November 2018